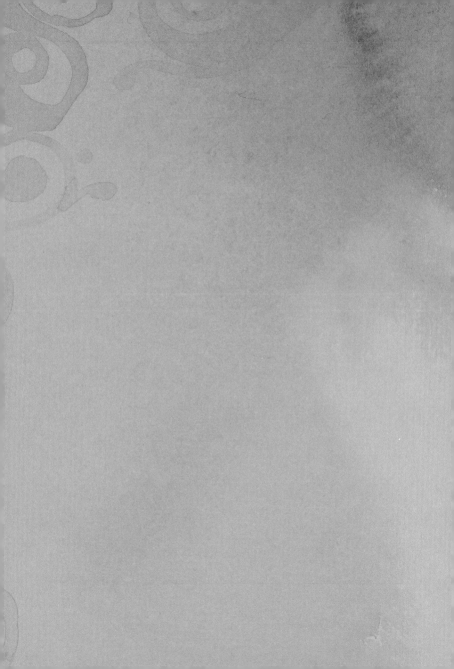

A GIFT FOR:

....

FROM:

....

Published by Hallmark Gift Books,
a division of Hallmark Cards, Inc.,
Kansas City, MO 64141
Visit us on the Web at Hallmark.com.

Original text by English poet and Anglican clergyman
John Newton (1725-1807)

Editorial Director: Delia Berrigan
Editor: Lindsay Evans
Art Director: Jan Mastin
Designer: Mark Voss
Production Designer: Bryan Ring

ISBN: 978-1-59530-702-6
1BOK2156

Printed and bound in China
JUN14

AMAZING GRACE

LYRICS YOU LOVE

Hallmark

Amazing grace!

HOW THE

SWEET SOUND

that SAVED a WRETCH like ME.

I once was lost,
but now am found,

'Twas grace that taught my heart to fear,

and grace my fears relieved.

How precious did that grace appear.

THE HOUR
I FIRST
Believe

Through many dangers,
toils, and snares

I HAVE ALREADY COME.

'Tis grace HAS brought ME safe thus far and grace WILL LEAD ME HOME.

The LORD
has promised
GOOD
to me—

His word, my hope secures.

He will my
shield and
portion be
as long as life

ENDURES.

Yea, when this flesh and heart shall fail and mortal life SHALL CEASE

I shall
within the
A Life of
and

possess

veil

Joy

Peace.

When we've been there

TEN THOUSAND
YEARS...

BRIGHT
SHINING
AS THE SUN...

WE'VE NO

TO SING

THAN WHEN

LESS DAYS
GOD'S PRAISE
WE'D FIRST BEGUN.

DID YOU ENJOY THIS BOOK?
WE WOULD LOVE TO HEAR FROM YOU.

Please send your comments to:
Hallmark Book Feedback
P.O. Box 419034
Mail Drop 100
Kansas City, MO 64141

Or e-mail us at:
booknotes@hallmark.com